ELSIE POOLE

THE ART OF INNER DIALOGUE

Mastering Self-Talk for Personal Growth
and Empowerment (2024 Guide for Beginners)

Copyright © 2023 by Elsie Poole

All rights reserved. No part of this publication may be reproduced, stored or transmitted in any form or by any means, electronic, mechanical, photocopying, recording, scanning, or otherwise without written permission from the publisher. It is illegal to copy this book, post it to a website, or distribute it by any other means without permission.

First edition

This book was professionally typeset on Reedsy.
Find out more at reedsy.com

Contents

1. Introduction — 1
2. Chapter 1: Understanding Self-Talk — 2
3. Exercise: 1 — 5
4. Chapter 2: Positive and Negative Self-Talk — 6
5. Exercise: 2 — 8
6. Chapter 3: The Consequences of Negative Self-Talk — 10
7. Exercise: 3 — 16
8. Chapter 4: The Power of Positive Self-Talk — 18
9. Exercise: 4 — 25
10. Chapter 5: Pareto's 80/20 Principle — 27
11. Chapter 6: Cultivating Optimal Conditions for Motivation — 31
12. Chapter 7: Understanding the Self — 34
13. Chapter 8: Embracing Self-Compassion — 36
14. Chapter 9: Exploring Your Inner Self — 39
15. Exercise: 5 — 44
16. Chapter 10: Who's Speaking? — 46
17. Exercise: 6 — 48
18. Chapter 11: The Significance of Pronouns — 49
19. Exercise: 7 — 51
20. Chapter 12: Embracing Silence — 52
21. Addendum: Specific Situations — 54

1

Introduction

Have you ever taken a moment to consider your internal dialogue? You know, that constant conversation that seems to endlessly play in your mind. It's the subtle voice in the background, articulating your thoughts, or rather, "speaking" them to you through an internal, or perhaps even infernal, commentary.

Or maybe you've brushed it off, never giving it much thought. But now that I've brought it up, I bet you're paying attention to it. Take a second to listen to your thoughts. More often than not, they're expressed in a mental voice. That's precisely what I'm referring to.

What prompts us to engage in silent or vocal self-talk? How does this inner dialogue influence our emotions and behaviors? "How can we become more conscious of the things we tell ourselves?"

These are intriguing queries, and we will delve into them shortly. However, the most valuable question we can ask is: Can we alter our self-talk? Is it possible to change the way we communicate with ourselves?

The answer is a resounding yes, we can. And that is the focal point of this book.

2

Chapter 1: Understanding Self-Talk

Let's begin by honing in on a precise definition. Self-talk, also known as intrapersonal communication, is the internal use of speech and language. It manifests as thoughts that you can "hear" within the auditory realm of your mind. It can also involve speaking to yourself aloud, a practice that is entirely normal, I assure you. Well, unless, of course, you're experiencing hallucinations or hearing voices, in which case it may signal a serious issue requiring the attention of a mental health professional. It's advisable, however, to refrain from vocalizing your thoughts when others are around. So, mumbling to yourself while walking down the street or perusing supermarket aisles might be best avoided.

Already, in the early stages of our discussion, you have practical advice on how to manage self-talk. You're welcome.

If you're still uncertain about what I mean, pay attention to your thoughts as you read these words silently. Do you "hear" the words in your mind as you read them? This, too, constitutes self-talk. For most individuals, the same inner voice is used to converse with oneself in various situations, virtually all the time.

Frequently, we don't consciously register our self-talk; it often acts as a half-conscious murmur at the edges of our awareness, akin to snippets of conversations in nearby cubicles at work. Yet, we all tune in to it regularly. This inner dialogue typically comments on ourselves, other people, and situations—whether past, present, or imagined future occurrences.

Imagine it as enabling the director's commentary on a movie; there's the actual movie, representing our experiences, and then there's the director's perspective, which mirrors our self-talk. Alternatively, it resembles a sports announcer providing commentary during a live game.

Upon careful observation, you'll notice that this internal dialogue mirrors your thoughts and emotions. Self-talk isn't arbitrary; it follows distinct patterns that repeat themselves. Everyone possesses their own unique self-talk patterns. Some people's self-talk revolves around the future, while others engage in internal dialogues about the past. Certain self-talk is positive and optimistic, while others are harsh, critical, or pessimistic. Sometimes, self-talk centers on people, and at other times, it fixates on objects or situations. It can oscillate between focusing mainly on others or oneself.

A recurring point we'll emphasize is the importance of paying attention to your self-talk and recognizing these patterns. By doing so, you can glean valuable insights into yourself. Identifying areas where your self-talk has a detrimental impact on your life is crucial. Once you're aware of this, you can intervene by altering the way you talk to yourself.

This awareness is vital because negative self-talk is intertwined with negative emotional states such as anxiety, depression, insecurity, rumination, and learned helplessness. It fosters a sense of overwhelming life circumstances, making it seem impossible to improve one's condition. Even if there were potential solutions, the belief in inevitable failure prevails. Clearly, this mindset is far from ideal.

Conversely, positive self-talk is correlated with reduced negative emotions and an increase in happiness, confidence, optimism, success, and a feeling of control and ownership over one's existence.

But how does this work? I posit that self-talk establishes a feedback loop. What you feed into it shapes what emerges, and your response to that outcome influences what you input the next time. By replacing negative inputs with positive ones, you disrupt a negative feedback loop, transforming it into a positive one. This sets off a chain reaction, akin to a snowball effect, which gains momentum. Make a small, positive change today, and it will gather force not only tomorrow but in the days that follow, until you find yourself astonished by your accomplishments.

3

Exercise: 1

Allocate some moments for self-reflection and focus on your inner dialogue. It's ideal to do this when you're not deeply engrossed in an activity. So, put away the ebook, set aside your devices, and take a leisurely walk in the park. Sit on your porch or balcony. Just spend some time alone and attune yourself to your internal conversation. Don't attempt to alter it; simply unwind and pay attention for now.

Repeat this exercise several times, and you'll soon begin to discern recurring patterns. Once you become accustomed to these patterns, try tuning in even when you're occupied with something else. Take note of what your inner voice is communicating as you work, socialize with friends, wash the dishes, or engage in any activity. This practice will provide you with insights into your self-talk tendencies across diverse situations.

This isn't merely a one-time activity; it's a valuable habit to cultivate within yourself. Initially, you may need to consciously make an effort, but over time, you'll naturally become aware of your self-talk without prompting.

4

Chapter 2: Positive and Negative Self-Talk

Let's revisit the sports commentary analogy mentioned earlier. A sports announcer assesses a player's performance during the game, offering criticism for mistakes or praise for exceptional plays. Similarly, your inner dialogue, or self-talk, continuously evaluates your actions and abilities. These evaluations can be either positive or negative. However, it's essential to understand that positive and negative self-talk doesn't merely relate to feeling good or feeling terrible about oneself. A more accurate distinction lies in categorizing them as constructive or dysfunctional.

Constructive self-talk involves thoughts that guide you toward your goals and support your personal growth. It empowers you to become a better version of yourself. On the other hand, dysfunctional self-talk traps you in unproductive, stagnant, repetitive patterns, especially if these patterns lead to feelings of misery and helplessness.

It's crucial to emphasize that negative emotions, or negative affect, are not inherently harmful. It's your interpretation of these emotions within your self-talk that determines their impact. For instance, researchers studying depression have identified a destructive self-talk pattern known as rumination. This involves obsessively dwelling on distressing symptoms without actively seeking solutions. In this scenario, negative emotions like sadness are compounded by toxic self-narratives, such as feeling utterly powerless and incapable of change.

Dysfunctional self-talk weaves a story—a detrimental one in which you are portrayed as passive and helpless.

In contrast, constructive self-talk paints a different narrative, one where you envision yourself as capable and resilient. This perspective not only boosts your mood but also acts as a self-fulfilling prophecy. If you perceive yourself as competent, you are more likely to embody that capability, placing you firmly in control of your life's direction.

With constructive self-talk, you might affirm:

- You've overcome challenges in the past with courage and hard work. You can overcome this one too.
    - Mistakes are a natural part of life; they don't define you. Learn from them and use that knowledge to move closer to your goals.
    - Your life is generally good, and you have the ability to make the necessary improvements. You are fully capable of handling what comes your way.
    - Acknowledge your achievements and take pride in your abilities. You deserve credit for your hard work, and it's okay to feel happy and proud when others recognize your accomplishments.

(You might have noticed the use of the second-person in these examples. There's a reason for this, which we'll explore shortly, but for now, I wanted to draw your attention to it.)

5

Exercise: 2

Maintain a journal or notepad with you, and create two lists titled "Constructive Self-Talk" and "Dysfunctional Self-Talk." Throughout your day or week, take note of both your positive and negative self-talk instances. Whenever you catch yourself engaging in negative self-talk, such as saying, "I'm always late" or "I'm not good enough," jot down those thoughts in the dysfunctional list. Similarly, when you find yourself engaging in positive self-talk, like "I can handle this challenge" or "I am capable of succeeding in this presentation," record those thoughts in the constructive list.

At the end of the day or week, review your lists. Reflect on the frequency of your positive and negative self-talk instances. How do you feel as you read through each list? Count the entries in each category and observe whether your self-talk leans more towards positivity or negativity. If negative self-talk dominates, there's no need to worry; we will discuss strategies to address this. If your self-talk is balanced or mostly positive, that's fantastic, but there's always room for improvement.

I intentionally left the timeframe open-ended to accommodate your schedule. If you have a busy routine and find it challenging to make notes every day, feel free to extend the exercise over a week or any duration that allows you to compile a substantial list of ten to twenty items.

EXERCISE: 2

Do not skip this exercise, and refrain from discarding your notes, as we will revisit them later in the process.

Chapter 3: The Consequences of Negative Self-Talk

Negative self-talk can have a range of detrimental effects on an individual. Primarily, it leads to a diminished sense of self-worth and is closely linked to feelings of anxiety, depression, stress, low self-esteem, and vulnerability. Furthermore, it can transform into a self-fulfilling prophecy, causing harm to one's performance and overall quality of life. A notable study discovered that even healthy teenagers of normal weight who merely perceived themselves as overweight were more likely to develop obesity in later years. Other research has demonstrated that negative self-talk can hinder performance in various aspects of life, from academic endeavors to professional roles and even recreational activities like playing darts.

Negative self-talk is particularly associated with elevated stress levels and difficulties in regulating emotions when confronted with stressful situations. Stress, a common experience for everyone, requires a more precise definition to truly grasp its nature. Stress can be defined as a set of physiological responses triggered by external factors. Physical manifestations of stress include muscle tension and pain, upper back, shoulder, and neck discomfort, increased heart rate, chest pain, elevated blood pressure, headaches, digestive issues like nausea, diarrhea, constipation, and ulcers, decreased libido, sexual function impairment, or impotence, insomnia, jaw tightness, teeth grinding (especially during sleep), sweating, and frequent illnesses (such as colds) due to a weakened immune system.

One theory posits that stress is essentially an evolutionary adaptation, akin to the fight-or-flight response. Our prehistoric ancestors relied on this response to deal with immediate threats in their natural environment. When faced with a predator, they would become hyper-alert, experiencing increased heart rate and a surge of adrenaline, preparing for either confrontation or rapid escape.

However, as human society evolved and shifted away from nature towards agriculture and urbanization, the complexity of our environment outpaced the development of our brains. We continued to rely on the same cognitive toolkit that served our hunter-gatherer ancestors. While survival was once dependent on hunting and gathering, our modern lives revolve around earning money by providing valuable goods or services. Consequently, anything jeopardizing our financial stability triggers a survival threat response. Additionally, in ancient times, survival was closely linked to belonging to a tribe, as banishment often led to death. Consequently, anything that severs our connections with family and friends, even if our financial resources are plentiful, is perceived as a threat to our survival.

Today, the threats and stressors in our environment are numerous and unceasing. The prospect of losing a job, missing out on a promotion, losing to a competitor, failing a course, experiencing financial losses, or making a social faux pas and facing social stigma all contribute to the constant stressors we encounter.

The challenge lies in the fact that the fight-or-flight response was adapted to address immediate and short-term threats, not prolonged and chronic ones. Consequently, we react to long-term stressors as if they were transient, which they are not. The physiological responses that accompany threats are advantageous in providing the energy and agility needed to evade immediate danger. However, if these responses persist over an extended period, they become detrimental. While short-term stress can have potential health benefits, chronic long-term stress leads to shorter and less healthy lives.

Negative self-talk amplifies this stress by distorting our perception of challenges and our ability to cope with them. Essentially, it magnifies everyday difficulties, making them appear more threatening than they truly are, thus intensifying stress further.

Negative self-talk employs several techniques to achieve this distortion. We can categorize these techniques into various cognitive distortions, including:

1. Catastrophizing:

This distortion involves blowing minor issues out of proportion, perceiving them as catastrophic events. For example, making a small mistake might be seen as a complete embarrassment, or spilling milk on the carpet might be considered a disaster.

2. Personalization:

This distortion involves automatically assuming that everything is related to oneself. For instance, if a boss forgets to include someone in an email, they might assume it's because of their poor performance, when in reality, it may have nothing to do with them.

3. Blaming:

Blaming can be directed either towards oneself or others. When blaming others, it's crucial to consider one's own role in the situation. Self-blame should be balanced with an acknowledgment that not everything is within one's control.

4. Filtering:

This distortion entails focusing solely on the negative aspects of a situation, ignoring any positive elements. For example, when facing relationship troubles, one might concentrate on their partner's flaws while neglecting their positive traits.

5. Overgeneralizing:

This involves drawing broad conclusions from isolated incidents. Failing once doesn't mean a person is a perpetual failure; it's important to recognize that each setback offers valuable lessons.

6. Black-or-White Thinking:

This distortion involves seeing situations as either completely positive or entirely negative, disregarding the many shades of gray in between.

These cognitive distortions are not an exhaustive list; there are additional types, such as jumping to conclusions, among others. They are fundamental elements of clinical approaches like cognitive-behavioral therapy, which seeks to address and correct these patterns of thinking.

At this point, you might wonder whether your negative self-talk is accurate. What if the negative assessment of yourself is correct? What if things genuinely are black and white, and you are indeed a failure?

First and foremost, it's crucial to recognize that terms like "failure" are value judgments, not objective facts. While value judgments play a vital role in decision-making, such as evaluating purchases, relationships, or ethical choices, they become detrimental when applied globally to oneself. You are, in essence, stuck with yourself, and you must work with the material you have. Therefore, indulging in self-criticism and harsh judgments can lead to hopelessness and hinder personal growth. Instead of blindly criticizing oneself, it's more productive to base assessments on factual information. Value judgments are only as valid as the facts they rest upon, so starting with a clear understanding of the situation and one's goals is essential. From there, one can formulate strategies for positive self-talk and life improvement.

Martin Seligman, a psychologist, conducted a significant experiment on classical conditioning involving dogs. He administered small electrical shocks to the dogs while ringing a bell. Over time, the dogs began to anticipate the shock even when the bell wasn't rung. In a subsequent test, Seligman placed the dogs in a partitioned room with one side electrified and the other not. Despite the low partition allowing them to escape, the dogs on the electrified side didn't attempt to jump over it. They passively endured the shocks, displaying a learned helplessness mentality. Even when he tested dogs that hadn't experienced previous shocks, they promptly jumped over the partition when shocked.

This phenomenon, named "learned helplessness," has been linked to depression-like symptoms in animals. Furthermore, individuals with learned helplessness struggle in problem-solving, have lower satisfaction in relationships and jobs, and often find themselves trapped in abusive relationships or poverty. This mental state hampers efforts to improve academic performance in some children. Learned helplessness fosters a belief that change is impossible, leading to persistent negative self-talk like "I can't" and "It's no use."

To break free from this detrimental mindset, it's essential to replace the victim script with positive self-talk. By challenging these negative beliefs and rewriting your internal dialogue, you can empower yourself to overcome learned helplessness and make positive changes in your life.

7

Exercise: 3

In your notebook, list the categories of negative self-talk:

1. Catastrophizing:

2. Personalization:

3. Blaming:

4. Filtering:

5. Overgeneralizing:

6. Black-or-White Thinking:

Leave space after each category for tally marks, as you will be keeping track of your thoughts.

Review your previous notes and consider each item of negative self-talk you identified. Categorize each thought into the appropriate cognitive distortion category. If a thought fits multiple categories, mark a point for each relevant category.

After analyzing your thoughts, observe which categories have the highest tally marks. These are the areas you need to focus on. For instance, if "Black-or-White Thinking" received the highest score, be vigilant about this pattern. Whenever you catch yourself engaging in negative self-talk, stop and either write it down or think about it systematically. Ask yourself the following questions:

1. Is this falling into a cognitive distortion, and if so, which one? Identify the distortion if possible.

2. What information or aspect of the situation might you be missing that's causing this perception?

3. What would be a more positive, accurate, and empowering perspective on this situation?

Although you might find it challenging to answer the last question initially, attempt to respond. We will delve into this in more detail in the next chapter.

Develop the habit of being mindful of your thoughts. Pay attention to the content of your mind, your thought patterns, and your self-talk. When you notice dysfunctional or distorting self-talk, interrogate it systematically. This process will enable you to discern whether there's substance behind these thoughts or if they are merely illusions.

Additionally, pay attention to your emotions during episodes of negative self-talk. Record your feelings—whether you feel happy, sad, nervous, confident, etc. Also, evaluate how these thoughts impact your actions and decisions. For instance, if you experienced negative self-talk about presenting an idea to your boss, document whether you went ahead with the presentation or if you retreated due to these thoughts.

8

Chapter 4: The Power of Positive Self-Talk

Positive self-talk offers a crucial advantage: it helps you steer clear of the pitfalls associated with negative self-talk. Although it might not initially seem like a significant benefit, considering the detrimental effects of negative self-talk—such as stress, anxiety, depression, rumination, and low self-esteem—it becomes apparent that its absence brings a silent, hidden positivity into your life.

Unlike negative experiences, the lack of negative emotions doesn't announce itself or leave a trace. You don't receive an email every morning celebrating the fact that your house hasn't burned down or that you haven't been engulfed by lava from a volcano. Acknowledging the absence of negativity is essential. Taking a moment to realize your good fortune, such as having functioning kidneys, allows you to appreciate the things you have and the challenges you've managed to avoid, preventing you from only recognizing their value when faced with their absence.

However, it's crucial to understand that the absence of negative emotions doesn't guarantee a constant state of cheerfulness. While the absence of negative emotions doesn't necessarily mean the presence of positive ones, the mere absence of negativity is a significant achievement in itself and is worth striving for.

It's important to note that practicing positive self-talk doesn't make you immune to stress or negative emotions. Life will still present challenges, and occasional stress is beneficial—it improves your health and longevity. Experiencing stress signifies that you are pushing yourself, stepping out of your comfort zone, and creating the necessary friction in your life to generate heat, energy, and growth. Embracing positive self-talk isn't about eliminating all challenges but equipping yourself with the mindset to navigate them with resilience and optimism.

Understanding Challenges: A Balance of Perception

The crucial distinction between positive and negative self-talk lies in how they interpret challenges:

Negative self-talk perceives stressors as threats

diminishing one's sense of control in the face of life's trials. It's akin to a dog surrendering to an electrified floor, lacking the will to overcome hurdles.

Positive self-talk views stressors as challenges

empowering individuals to take control of their narrative, actively shaping their lives amid adversities. Embracing positive self-talk means asserting your agency, continuously evolving, and constructing a resilient self.

However, achieving the right balance is essential. Entirely avoiding challenges results in a superficial existence centered on momentary pleasures, akin to living as a child. Conversely, tackling insurmountable challenges often leads to failure, eroding confidence and hindering personal growth. Striking a balance, similar to tuning a guitar string, is crucial. Challenges should be significant enough to foster growth but not so overwhelming that failure becomes inevitable.

Your emotions serve as indicators of this equilibrium. Facing challenges at an appropriate level results in positive, attentive, and engaged feelings, signifying the importance of your efforts. Pushing too hard leads to panic and overwhelm, while being too lenient causes initial boredom, evolving into a pervasive sense of unease, dread, and the feeling of wasting life.

Recognizing this balance is vital. Your mind is an instrument; akin to a musician, regularly and adeptly tune it. Stay attuned to your emotions, adjusting your approach as needed to maintain this delicate equilibrium.

Self-Leadership Revisited

In a study conducted in 2013, both effective and ineffective senior executives were asked to draft letters to their future selves. These letters served as a window into the executives' self-talk patterns. The researchers also linked effective leadership to robust self-leadership, emphasizing qualities such as discipline, self-management, and a willingness to tackle inherently motivating challenges. Essentially, self-leadership aligns closely with the concept of self-agency we previously discussed: the act of taking control of one's own life and decisions.

The study defined positive or constructive self-talk as involving "accurate self-analysis, well-founded beliefs, and an optimistic outlook," while negative self-talk was characterized by "dwelling on and fixating on the negative aspects of challenging situations." Notably, the study found that effective leaders, those exhibiting strong self-leadership, demonstrated positive self-talk in their self-addressed letters. Moreover, positive self-talk was positively linked to creativity and problem-solving skills. These leaders composed letters to their future selves that were not just motivational but also self-compassionate, contemplative, and insightful.

Positive self-talk was closely linked to enhanced leadership qualities and reduced work-related stress. Conversely, negative self-talk was associated with weaker leadership skills and diminished creativity and problem-solving abilities. Unlike managers with a negative self-talk mindset who perceived problems as daunting obstacles, those with positive self-talk regarded challenges as opportunities for growth and development.

Navigating Positive Self-Talk: A Balance of Realism

You might be skeptical about positive self-talk, thinking it involves merely cheering yourself on or engaging in superficial affirmations. You might wonder if it's just a form of self-deception. Is it not akin to lying to oneself?

The truth is, positive self-talk isn't about pretending or fabricating abilities or achievements that don't exist. Think of it as avoiding the trap of false positivity, akin to a misleading result on a diagnostic test. Falling into this trap can make you believe you've attained a goal when you haven't, ultimately hindering your actual progress.

Consider a scenario: you're overweight, acknowledging the need for change. Negative self-talk berates you, making you feel helpless. Conversely, false positivity attempts to convince you that everything is fine, but deep down, you recognize the deception.

In the realm of true positive self-talk, honesty prevails. You admit your current state but specify your desired goal clearly. For instance, acknowledging, "I want to lose ten pounds, and I know how to achieve it," reflects this genuine positivity. In this approach, you neither deceive nor criticize yourself. Instead, you acknowledge reality, outline your objective, and express confidence in your ability to reach your goals.

Genuine positivity involves being realistic about your situation, defining your objectives clearly, and having confidence in your capacity to achieve them. This aligns with the constructive self-talk defined in the earlier study: "accurate self-analysis, well-grounded beliefs, and an encouraging orientation."

Illustrations of Inner Dialogue

By now, you grasp the concept, but let's delve into specific examples to enhance your understanding. Examining concrete instances can offer clearer insights into the concept of self-talk.

Negative: If I contribute in this meeting, I might say something foolish and embarrass myself in front of the higher-ups. I should just stay silent.

Positive: You possess interesting and valuable ideas to share. By expressing them, the higher-ups can assess their worth. If they appreciate them, great! If not, it's no loss on your part. Taking a chance can lead to potential gains.

Negative: My hobby is just a casual pursuit; I'm only an amateur. Displaying my creations to strangers would be embarrassing.

Positive: Your non-work interests could captivate others too. Showcase your ideas and creations; you might connect with intriguing, like-minded individuals who aid your growth. Who knows, this passion could even evolve into a business venture. You won't know until you try.

Negative: I can't believe he didn't return my call. He must be ignoring me and doesn't respect me.

Positive: Perhaps something significant cropped up, or he's overwhelmed and hasn't had the chance to respond. It's essential to give it more time before jumping to conclusions.

Negative: She constantly nags about trivial matters. I'm fed up with her pettiness.

Positive: Yes, her overreactions are vexing, but let's face it: everyone overreacts occasionally. Overreaction isn't her sole trait; she contributes in many ways too. Attempting a calm conversation, understanding her concerns, and finding a resolution might be beneficial.

Negative: I'm too busy to learn a musical instrument.

Positive: You decide how to use your time outside work. If it matters to you, allocate some time for practice, even if it's just 15 minutes.

Observing these examples, it becomes apparent that they aren't grounded in facts but in subjective value judgments. These judgments, positive or negative, are not inherently true or false. The crucial inquiry isn't about their accuracy but their utility. Are they valuable? Do they motivate or hinder? Positive self-talk is not blindly optimistic; it's a realistic analysis, exploring life's nuances practically. It engages in creative problem-solving and aids in making sound decisions.

The differentiating factor between positive and negative self-talk lies not in factual content but in the interpretation of situations. This interpretation carries emotional weight and dictates the approach, whether passive or active, constructive or dysfunctional. Remember, most thoughts, whether positive or negative, are subjective. The key question about self-talk remains: Is it uplifting you or pulling you down?

To summarize, positive self-talk offers numerous advantages, not only by eliminating the harmful impacts of negative self-talk but also by providing its own set of positive benefits, including:

1. Enhanced motivation
2. A willingness to view challenges as opportunities
3. Increased feelings of self-control and self-mastery
4. Self-compassion and self-nurturing
5. Boosted creativity
6. Improved problem-solving abilities

9

Exercise: 4

Certainly, implementing positive self-talk is a transformative process that requires continuous effort and self-awareness. To actively counter negative self-talk, follow these steps:

1. Identify Negative Thoughts: Whenever you catch yourself engaging in negative self-talk, jot down the thought in your journal. Pay special attention to the cognitive distortions you identified earlier.

2. Analyze the Thought: Break down the negative thought. Determine what part of it is factual and what part is a value judgment or interpretation.

3. Reframe the Thought Positively: Write down a more constructive version of the thought. Focus on making it motivating, encouraging, self-empathic, and solution-oriented. Ask yourself the three questions: Is this a cognitive distortion? What am I missing? What would be a more positive, accurate, and empowering way to view this situation?

4. Keep a Running List: Maintain an ongoing list of negative thoughts you encounter throughout the day. Rewrite each of them in a positive and constructive manner. Affirm your agency in these rephrased statements.

5. Observe Your Feelings and Actions: Pay attention to how changing your self-talk affects your emotions and behavior. Notice if your mood improves and if you become more proactive in pursuing your goals.

6. **Practice Positive Self-Talk:** Cultivate the habit of generating positive self-talk in your mind, especially during challenging situations. This mental practice can be just as effective as writing it down.

Remember, the goal is to gradually shift your internal dialogue from self-limiting and negative to empowering and positive. With consistent effort and self-reflection, you can reshape your thought patterns and enhance your overall well-being.

10

Chapter 5: Pareto's 80/20 Principle

When glancing at your list from Chapter 2 and encountering a slew of negative items, it's easy to feel disheartened. Thoughts might flood your mind, convincing you of the futility of the situation, making you believe you're trapped in a sea of negativity. But pause for a moment and analyze that thought. Is it grounded in reality? While negative thoughts might dominate your mind, that doesn't signify an insurmountable hurdle. It's a projection, not a fact—an erroneous prediction lacking substantiating evidence. Instead, remind yourself: yes, negative thoughts abound, but transforming oneself was never meant to be effortless. Begin with small steps, addressing the issue gradually. Eventually, progress will manifest.

Economics provides a compelling explanation through the Pareto principle, a concept illustrating unequal distributions. Vilfredo Pareto, an Italian economist, observed that 80% of Italy's land was owned by just 20% of its populace, while the remaining 80% of the people possessed only 20% of the land—a phenomenon now recognized as the Pareto distribution. Remarkably, this pattern extends universally. Most quantifiable aspects of human society and creative endeavors adhere to this 80/20 rule: approximately 80% of effects stem from 20% of causes.

In economies, around 20% of the population often commands 80% of the wealth, accentuating income inequality. Similarly, within a sales team, roughly 20% of salespeople close 80% of deals, and 20% of products generate about 80% of sales. Even the natural world adheres to this principle; 20% of pea plants yield 80% of the peas, showcasing its ubiquity.

Consider Google Scholar, a platform for academic articles, where citations propel papers to the top. This led to a Pareto effect: the most cited papers garner even more citations, while the bottom ones languish, resulting in an extreme 80/20 distribution.

Economists term this phenomenon the Matthew effect, wherein the affluent amass more wealth, and the impoverished struggle further. Yet, there's hope in understanding this principle. By harnessing the Matthew effect, you can turn it to your advantage.

Both the Matthew effect and the Pareto distribution underscore life's inherent imbalance, driven by momentum. As psychologist Jordan Peterson emphasizes, consistent self-improvement, no matter how minor, accumulates. Each improvement serves as a foundation for the next, culminating in exponential ease of progress. "For to everyone who has, more shall be given." This transformation isn't instantaneous; it's an accumulation, a gradual ascent from the 80% to the 20%.

CHAPTER 5: PARETO'S 80/20 PRINCIPLE

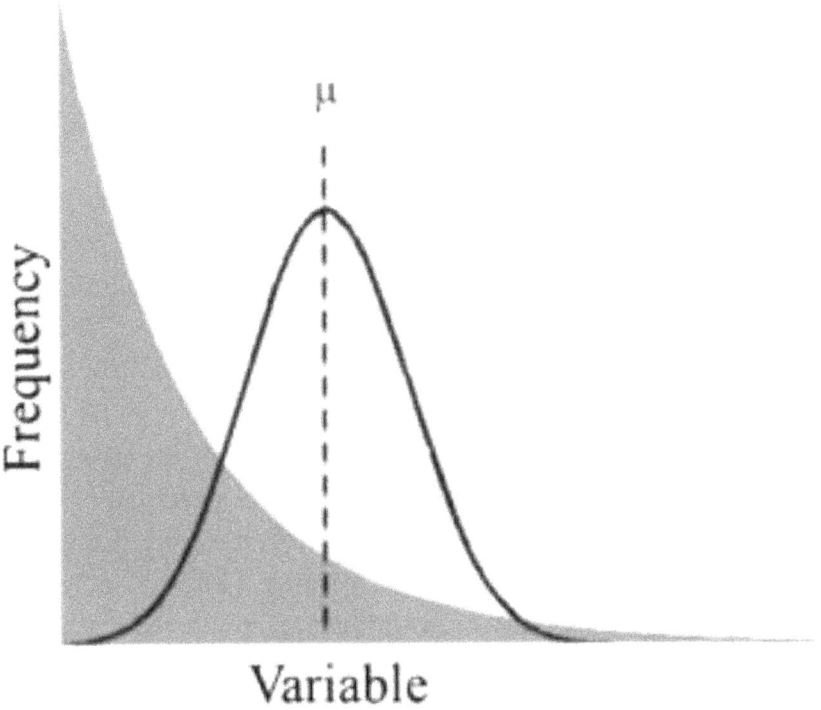

I mentioned that accumulation happens gradually, and in a certain sense, it does, but its effects remain mostly imperceptible until suddenly they're not. This phenomenon is evident from the shape of the Pareto distribution depicted in the image above. There's a subtle, gradual rise—so gradual that it might escape notice, akin to watching a plant grow. Then, growth takes an abrupt, dramatic turn.

Nature, as evidenced by numerous examples, doesn't progress steadily; rather, it moves in leaps and bounds. Evolution, for instance, occurs in punctuated equilibria, with species remaining stable until an environmental change triggers rapid adaptation. Even at the quantum level, electrons change states suddenly—a phenomenon known as the quantum leap. Zooming out to the macro level, similar patterns emerge in the stock market. Stocks accumulate, experiencing sideways movements before suddenly embarking on an upward trend.

In personal development, progress unfolds in plateaus and sharp ascents. One must endure the accumulation phase before witnessing an upward trajectory. During this period, around 80% of individuals succumb to discouragement due to the lack of visible progress. Without tangible results, doubt creeps in, leading many to quit.

Yet, the remaining 20% persevere through the accumulation phase with unwavering determination. In the long run, the efforts of these resolute and disciplined individuals yield substantial rewards.

The pivotal question is: Do you want to belong to the majority— the eighty percent—or the determined minority—the twenty percent? The encouraging news is that by practicing the exercises outlined in this book, you're already progressing along the Pareto distribution. Each time you reframe your self-talk in a positive manner, reducing negative emotions, enhancing positive ones, and reinforcing your sense of authorship over your life, you're constructing the staircase, brick by brick. Eventually, the staircase appears to build itself, almost miraculously, as your efforts accumulate.

Chapter 6: Cultivating Optimal Conditions for Motivation

In the preceding chapter, we delved into the idea of gradual progress, following the Pareto principle, and the frustration that arises when our advancements often go unnoticed. Expanding on this notion, let's explore the concept of motivation.

Motivation isn't a static force; it ebbs and flows. What was once a robust drive can wane if you feel your efforts lead nowhere. Conversely, a feeble motivation can gain strength unexpectedly, spurred by unexpected rewards, be it pleasure, financial gain, or other forms of gratification.

The intensity of motivation hinges significantly on the anticipation of rewards, although not exclusively. Belief in a cause or idea can be equally compelling. Sometimes, you invest your energy not for personal gain, but because you genuinely believe in the significance of your actions; you perceive them as part of a greater purpose, something larger than yourself.

Motivation also falls into two categories: intrinsic and extrinsic. Let me elucidate. In a conventional job, you dedicate your time and labor, receiving regular payment in return. Even if you genuinely enjoy your work, the primary impetus remains external—a paycheck. This external drive can even take a negative form; you might attend work unwillingly to avoid the consequences of absenteeism.

Consider volunteering at a food bank or homeless shelter. Your motivation springs from an internal well of compassion and a desire to alleviate the suffering of others. It's an inherent drive, intrinsic and altruistic. Similarly, spending a Saturday engrossed in video games, purely for the joy it brings, represents intrinsic motivation. The reward lies in the inherent satisfaction derived from the activity itself.

Intrinsic motivation generally prevails because the activity itself is inherently fulfilling; the satisfaction it provides is the reward. Extrinsic motivation, on the other hand, necessitates constant reminders of why you're pursuing a certain path, as the rewards might be delayed or external.

Yet, motivation is complex; it can clash and create dilemmas. Imagine you're passionate about collecting My Little Pony toys, but societal norms discourage such interests in adults. Here, your intrinsic motivation—to pursue a hobby you love—conflicts with extrinsic pressures to conform to societal expectations.

In situations like these, navigating conflicting motivations can be challenging, especially when embarking on self-improvement, such as the journey you're on by reading this book and altering your self-talk. It becomes a litmus test for your relationships. Genuine friends support and encourage your growth, celebrating your victories without envy. In contrast, false friends exhibit strange reactions to your successes, displaying jealousy or attempting to diminish your achievements. For instance, if you're trying to quit smoking, fake friends might offer you cigarettes; if you're striving to quit drinking, they might coax you into having "just one beer." Similarly, when you start a new relationship, they might criticize your partner or fuel unwarranted suspicions about their faithfulness. Recognizing genuine support amidst such challenges is key to sustaining your motivation and self-improvement efforts.

It might be subtle, but if you're working on improving your mindset with positive self-talk, some people will notice the change and counter it by filling your thoughts with negativity to breed doubt. It's crucial to identify such individuals, especially during self-improvement efforts, as when you strive to rise, there will be those aiming to pull you down.

However, social pressure isn't entirely negative; it can actually enhance your motivation. Bad days happen to everyone, whether due to specific unfortunate events or just feeling off. During these times, having a true friend around can lift your spirits when self-encouragement falters.

Leveraging social pressure involves two key strategies. First, surround yourself with positive people. Negative company breeds negative thoughts, while positive companions encourage empowering self-talk, shaping your perception of yourself. Secondly, share your goals with friends. If you announce your intentions, caring friends will inquire about your progress, motivating you to stay committed. The fear of disappointing them can provide the extra push needed during moments of weak motivation.

However, social pressure has its pitfalls. Consider a determined novelist constantly working on his book, surrounded by relatives who subtly criticize his progress and compare him to his successful cousin. Under such scrutiny, maintaining motivation requires immense strength. To safeguard your motivation, avoid environments where it might be undermined. Strengthen your self-confidence internally; otherwise, the external negativity could turn into damaging self-talk, undermining your efforts.

Don't fight against the current when changing your attitude and life. Instead, choose a social environment that maximizes motivation. Your mind will naturally follow suit, fostering positive, encouraging, and empowering thoughts effortlessly.

12

Chapter 7: Understanding the Self

All of us carry an internal perception of ourselves, an identity that shapes who we believe we are. We casually use words like "I" and "me" without delving into their deeper meanings. For many, the concept of self remains unexamined and seemingly straightforward—we are who we are, no questions asked.

However, the reality is far more intricate. As humans, we've evolved with a sense of self, but understanding why this belief in self exists and its practical purpose raises intriguing questions. What function does self-perception serve, especially in the context of self-talk? If self-talk is indeed an evolutionary trait, it's distinctly human, rooted in our ability to communicate internally. But dissecting the brain won't reveal a specific "self" region; instead, it emerges from intricate interactions among various brain parts.

The self, contrary to intuition, isn't a singular, stable entity but an amalgamation of neurological and psychological processes. From a psychological standpoint, self-talk connects to how you perceive yourself, others, and stressful events, functioning as an internal dialogue. This ability for internal conversations appears abstract but finds its roots in our evolutionary need to anticipate scenarios not unfolding in the present moment.

Consider the act of mentally exploring potential situations—whether swimming in a river teeming with crocodiles or investing in cryptocurrency. These mental simulations help us evaluate risks and rewards without exposing ourselves to real dangers. This process involves extensive mental imagery and self-dialogue, narrating a story of our journey from past experiences (point A) to future aspirations (point B), which represent our goals.

Positive self-talk fuels empowerment, aiding goal attainment, while negative self-talk hampers progress. Thus, negative self-talk fails in fulfilling its evolutionary purpose. Self-talk functions due to our ability to simulate scenarios mentally and our language capacity. To simulate, we project an image of ourselves, creating a separation between our present selves and the imagined versions. Simultaneously, our evolved linguistic skills enable sophisticated communication, facilitating internal dialogue.

Combining these aspects—mental distance between real and projected selves and our innate inclination to communicate—results in self-talk. This internal dialogue proves valuable, akin to conversations with others, offering critical self-reflection and diverse perspectives. However, the efficacy of self-talk hinges on the nature of the perspective communicated. Empowering self-talk enhances its utility, optimizing its potential, while disempowering self-talk proves not just useless but detrimental. Therefore, the quality of the internal dialogue profoundly influences its impact on our lives.

13

Chapter 8: Embracing Self-Compassion

Reflect on the instances of negative self-talk, both those you've experienced and those outlined in this book. Notice the harshness and criticism in this internal dialogue—how you shoot down your ideas, erode your confidence, and openly insult yourself. Strangely, this self-criticism can be remarkably cruel, akin to how someone might treat you if they harbored strong animosity toward you.

Consider this: there are individuals in the world who treat others with kindness and compassion but fail to extend the same courtesy to themselves. Ask yourself, would you speak to someone you love in the same harsh manner you sometimes use on yourself? Likely not. Genuine love involves encouragement and support, acknowledging achievements without inflating false hopes or concealing harsh realities. You empower your loved ones with motivating words, helping them pursue meaningful goals and take charge of their lives.

So why don't you afford yourself the same kindness? Whether you're a parent, spouse, sibling, relative, or close friend, someone in your life loves you deeply. Imagine how it would distress them to know that you harbor an internal voice that belittles you and undermines your well-being. Therefore, the fundamental principle for fostering positive self-talk is simple yet profound:

Speak to yourself with the same compassion you would offer someone you love deeply.

Understanding Emotional Intelligence

Emotional intelligence, a concept popularized by Daniel Goleman, refers to the ability to perceive and manage both your own emotions and the emotions of others. It is closely tied to empathy, as empathy enables us to not only recognize others' feelings but also genuinely care about them. Self-empathy, or self-love, involves acknowledging your own emotions and nurturing your emotional well-being.

This book focuses on enhancing your emotional intelligence throughout its entirety. Techniques such as identifying cognitive distortions present in negative self-talk and replacing them with positive and empowering self-talk are fundamental aspects of this process. In the upcoming chapter, we will explore understanding your personality traits, another crucial element of emotional intelligence. The aim of this chapter is to emphasize the importance of developing emotional intelligence by cultivating self-compassion and recognizing your feelings, much like you would for a loved one.

For further insights into emotional intelligence, detailed information can be found in my book, "Emotional Intelligence Training: A Practical Guide to Understanding Your Emotions and Enhancing Your EQ," available on the Kindle Store. I encourage you to explore its contents for a deeper understanding of this topic.

Present and Future Selves: A New Perspective on the Golden Rule

You're likely familiar with the Golden Rule: treat others as you want to be treated, understanding their desires and avoiding their suffering. But there's a lesser-known version of this rule: treat your future self as you would your present self. Oddly, many people view their future selves as entirely separate entities from their current selves.

In a study, psychologists at Princeton asked participants to decide how much of an unpleasant concoction they would drink. Those choosing for themselves opted for a small amount, while those deciding for another participant selected larger quantities. Surprisingly, when asked to choose for themselves two weeks in the future, participants picked larger amounts, treating their future selves as strangers. This phenomenon sheds light on why people often prioritize short-term rewards over long-term gains and why procrastination occurs. Delaying tasks with distant rewards seems acceptable because, mentally, the future feels like someone else's problem.

Considering the future is a high-level abstraction, unique to humans. Unlike other animals, we possess advanced abilities to plan and prepare, imagining events yet to occur. However, our focus tends to be on the present due to its immediate reality, while the future, being abstract, takes a backseat. Our inclination towards instant gratification aligns with our evolutionary history, making us favor immediate rewards over distant, uncertain outcomes.

In essence, our brains, built on ancient systems, struggle to embrace the artificial concept of the future fully. This cognitive bias leads us to prioritize short-term rewards, often neglecting behaviors with delayed benefits that might never materialize.

Chapter 9: Exploring Your Inner Self

Navigating the OCEAN of Personality

The realm of personality is a substantial domain under scrutiny within the field of psychology. The quantification of personality is formally referred to as psychometrics. Within psychometrics, one of the extensively researched subjects is the Big Five personality traits. These encompass openness, conscientiousness, extraversion, agreeableness, and neuroticism, forming a convenient mnemonic: OCEAN or CANOE.

Openness

denotes an inclination toward novelty, encompassing attributes such as curiosity, imagination, and an insatiable drive to acquire new knowledge and explore uncharted territories. Individuals with high scores in openness tend to exhibit a keen appreciation for the realms of art, ideas, and literature. They often exhibit creativity and possess expansive vocabularies compared to those with lower openness scores. Furthermore, they tend to embrace unique, even eccentric beliefs and lean towards political liberalism. Conversely, individuals scoring lower in openness demonstrate a preference for practicality over novelty and abstraction, emphasizing the importance of "just the facts." In extreme cases, they may tend towards dogmatism.

Conscientiousness

on the other hand, pertains to qualities of orderliness and industriousness. Those with high conscientiousness are characterized by tidiness, meticulous organization, discipline, industriousness, and adherence to conventional norms. They excel as planners and maintain a low tolerance for idleness and poor hygiene in others. Politically, they often lean toward conservatism. In contrast, individuals with low conscientiousness may exhibit disorganization and messiness but also possess flexibility and spontaneity.

It is crucial to recognize that conscientiousness and openness are not diametrically opposed; one can exhibit traits of both or neither.

Extraversion

revolves around an orientation towards external activities and interactions with people (in contrast to introversion, which favors introspection and less social engagement). Extroverts draw energy and experience heightened positive emotions from engaging with the external world. They are typically high-energy individuals who radiate enthusiasm when in the company of others. Introverts, conversely, engage in fewer social interactions and prefer quieter pursuits. It is important to note that introversion does not equate to shyness, as introverts may not readily display their excitement and often possess a more independent disposition.

Agreeableness

encompasses sensitivity to the feelings of others and a desire for harmony and cooperation. Agreeable individuals tend to establish rapport with others effortlessly, exhibiting kindness, compassion, and a helpful nature. They are quick to offer compromises and consider the interests of those around them. In contrast, those with low agreeableness are not necessarily unkind but are more inclined to stand their ground and are unafraid of conflict. Their self-interest may sometimes lead to uncooperative and suspicious behavior. Nonetheless, their resolute nature proves invaluable when defending critical causes. In team dynamics, not everyone can embody the traits of Bruce Banner; someone has to be the Hulk.

Neuroticism

the last trait on this list, characterizes a disposition towards negative emotions, particularly anxiety, anger, depression, and insecurity. Individuals with high neuroticism scores are emotionally less stable and exhibit lower impulse control, possessing a diminished tolerance for stress. Conversely, those with low neuroticism scores maintain emotional stability, experiencing fewer negative emotions. This does not necessarily imply an abundance of positive emotions; rather, they possess a higher stress tolerance and are less prone to irritability, depression, vulnerability, and anxiety.

Understanding your placement on the Big Five traits is essential for genuine personal growth. Recognizing your strengths and weaknesses enhances self-awareness. It's crucial to grasp that traits labeled negatively, such as disagreeableness, aren't inherently bad. Disagreeable individuals are courageous in conflicts; they resist manipulation and confront those who deceive them.

Considerable data links personality with various life aspects. For instance, conscientiousness significantly predicts success in academics and work, a consistent finding across multiple studies. Conversely, neuroticism is a negative predictor.

But how does this relate to self-talk? This question is pivotal. To improve your self-talk, understanding your personality is key. Identifying areas for enhancement is half the battle; psychometrics offer a potent tool for formulating problems effectively.

Personality, although generally stable, can change over time, influenced by age and conscious effort. Recognizing your personality traits informs your self-talk. For instance, high neuroticism often leads to negative, self-critical thoughts. Too much focus on self-talk can exacerbate this trait.

Armed with this knowledge, activities like mindfulness, sports, or martial arts can redirect your attention from negative self-talk. Similarly, a high agreeableness score prompts reflection on relationships; are others as considerate as you are? Evaluating your self-talk during conflicts reveals whether you prioritize your needs appropriately.

Disagreeable people often fare better in the workplace, earning more due to assertive negotiation. Positive, assertive self-talk can aid in seeking a raise or promotion confidently.

Decreasing negative self-talk reduces negative emotions, but cultivating positive emotions is linked to extraversion. Introverts can enhance positive emotion through increased social engagement. Positive self-talk, encouraging oneself to participate and emphasizing personal value, boosts confidence and energy in social interactions.

In essence, understanding your personality traits provides insight into your self-talk patterns. Tailoring self-talk can lead to positive changes in your thoughts, emotions, and actions, creating a harmonious feedback loop for personal growth.

15

Exercise: 5

Taking a Big Five personality test provides valuable insights into your character. To discover your traits, you can utilize the comprehensive test at understandmyself.com, designed by qualified psychologists, or opt for a quicker and free alternative at psychologytoday.com/tests/personality/big-five-personality-test. Once you have your scores, engage in a reflective writing exercise for each trait.

For **openness**, recall a situation where your pragmatism served you well and another instance where your lack of interest in new experiences caused you to miss out. Analyze what you could have done differently and envision better outcomes.

For **conscientiousness**, reflect on a time when your meticulous planning led to success and another occasion where your strictness hindered your flexibility. Consider alternative approaches and envision a more balanced response.

Regarding **extraversion**, think about a moment when your social engagement brought positivity into your life and another occasion where your introversion kept you from seizing an opportunity. Ponder on how you could have embraced social situations with confidence.

Consider **agreeableness**; recall an instance when your kindness strengthened a relationship and another situation where being overly agreeable led to exploitation. Imagine setting boundaries and expressing your needs assertively.

Lastly, for **neuroticism**, reflect on a time when your sensitivity to emotions helped you navigate a difficult situation and another moment when excessive worrying caused unnecessary stress. Contemplate on adopting a more resilient mindset.

Review your reflections and pinpoint one or two traits you wish to improve. Develop affirmations tailored to these traits, ensuring they are concise, memorable, and empowering. Incorporate these affirmations into your daily routine, reinforcing positive self-talk. In challenging situations, mentally repeat these affirmations to guide your thoughts toward a more constructive path:

- "I embrace new experiences with curiosity and enthusiasm."
    - "I balance my planning with adaptability, finding the middle ground."
    - "I confidently engage in social interactions, embracing connections."
    - "I express kindness while setting boundaries, valuing my needs."
    - "I maintain emotional resilience, focusing on solutions rather than worries."

By integrating these affirmations into your self-talk, you empower yourself to navigate life's challenges with a more positive and resilient mindset.

16

Chapter 10: Who's Speaking?

For many, the inner dialogue feels like their own voice—a conversation with oneself. During these moments, it's common to perceive this self-talk as a personal dialogue. And in a way, it is. However, as we explored earlier, the "self" we often regard as a singular, continuous "I" is, in fact, a sophisticated network of neurological processes—a community within a single person, as described by psychologist Charles Fernyhough, the author of The Voices Within: The History and Science of How We Talk to Ourselves. Inner speech, a topic of new scientific inquiry, reveals itself as a far-reaching, multi-perspective conversation.

Imagine this self as akin to a computer—not a solitary entity but a complex assembly of psychological programs. When hunger strikes, a program activates, urging you to seek sustenance. Another program, related to reproduction, stirs in the presence of a tempting mating opportunity. And when danger looms, a fight-or-flight program springs into action, flooding your body with adrenaline, preparing you for combat or swift escape.

These programs operate akin to the background processes in a computer, hidden from view while the user interacts with the screen. The user interface, much like our perception of a coherent self, offers a limited perspective. Higher cognitive functions, problem-solving, and narrative construction are part of these more advanced programs. The notion of "I did this" or "I fought" emerges only after these processes are well underway—a convenient fiction we construct.

But what if we could tell ourselves a different story? Currently, a major flaw in this narrative is the tendency to equate negative self-talk with the essence of oneself. If you tell yourself, "I'm stupid," you're implying that stupidity defines you. Yet, fundamentally, this isn't the truth. As Walt Whitman aptly expressed, "I am large. I contain multitudes."

Negative self-identifications stem from learned helplessness, a flawed mental pattern. However, changing this pattern isn't as simple as uninstalling a program—it's deeply ingrained. Instead, consider a different approach: view negative self-talk as a pesky relative you encounter during holidays—annoying yet harmless. Give it a name, imagine it as a bothersome voice. When it intrudes, remind yourself, "Oh, Uncle Vernon is rambling again."

This strategy introduces a crucial gap between negative self-talk and your identity. By distancing yourself from the inner critical voice, its power diminishes. It becomes just another noise in the background, no more significant than any other distraction.

This principle forms the basis for the next chapter's discussion.

17

Exercise: 6

Review the content you documented in Chapter 2, where you recorded both your positive and negative self-talk. We'll focus on the negative self-talk list.

Picture a character, someone you can associate with your negative self-talk. It's more effective if this character is comical and amusing rather than hostile or intimidating. This way, it becomes an object of mockery that you can find humor in.

Rephrase each thought or piece of self-talk as if it were spoken by this character. Consider how you would respond if someone with this comical persona said those things to you. Document your replies as well.

By doing this, you'll be equipped to swiftly apply the naming technique in your ongoing inner dialogue. Dedicate some time, whether it's a day, two days, or a week, to practice naming your self-talk using this approach. Pay attention to any shifts in your emotions, your self-confidence, and your overall experiences in different aspects of your life.

18

Chapter 11: The Significance of Pronouns

In the previous chapter, we discussed how recognizing your negative self-talk as someone else's voice can create distance, preventing you from associating it too closely with your own identity.

This chapter explores a simple mental trick that achieves a similar effect from a different angle. Allow me to explain further. Take a moment to reflect on your self-talk patterns. What pronouns do you typically use? Most likely, you employ first-person singular pronouns like "I," "me," "my," and "mine."

Recent research suggests that employing non-first-person pronouns can be more beneficial. Instead of addressing yourself as "I," try using second-person pronouns like "you," or third-person pronouns such as "he" or "she." Alternatively, you can refer to yourself by your own name: "Come on, Julie, you can do it," or "Take it easy, Dan, don't overreact."

A famous instance of this technique occurred when LeBron James changed teams in 2010. He explained, "I didn't want to make an emotional decision. I wanted to do what was best for LeBron James and what LeBron James was going to do to make him happy." While it might have seemed odd at the time, speaking about oneself in the second or third person is a proven method to emotionally distance oneself from a situation, aiding in better decision-making. This approach is supported by robust research.

Similar to the method discussed in the previous chapter, this technique creates emotional separation between you and your thoughts, enhancing emotional regulation and self-control. Non-first-person self-talk facilitates self-distancing or de-centering, enabling individuals to objectively assess irrational thoughts and observe their feelings without being overwhelmed by them. Additionally, it reduces stress and anxiety in social scenarios. Studies have demonstrated that individuals who engaged in non-first-person self-talk experienced less anxiety and performed better in public speaking and making favorable first impressions. Furthermore, this method helps individuals perceive future stressful situations as challenges they are capable of handling, rather than threats.

Cutting-edge studies, less than four years old, utilized brain imaging to explore the impact of different self-talk approaches on negative memories. Participants were instructed to reflect on negative memories using first-person pronouns ("I" and "me") or non-first-person pronouns. The results revealed that the group using non-first-person pronouns exhibited reduced brain activity associated with emotional reactions while displaying enhanced cognitive control.

This groundbreaking psychological research offers significant therapeutic potential for empowering individuals to take control of their lives. It is an invaluable discovery for those engaged in personal development, as it provides a relatively effortless way to achieve self-control and emotional regulation by simply altering the way we talk to ourselves, using second or third person pronouns.

19

Exercise: 7

Once again, revisit the lists you created in Chapter 2. However, this time, rephrase the items without incorporating first-person pronouns.

Consider this a preparatory step before implementing the third-person technique in real-life situations. Yes, you guessed it right – it's time to put this into practice. Channel your inner LeBron James.

And remember to assess the outcomes: How does it impact your emotions? Your behavior? Your performance?

20

Chapter 12: Embracing Silence

We've delved into the drawbacks of negative self-talk and the benefits of positive self-talk extensively. While it's crucial to practice positive self-talk, it's equally important not to confine your focus solely within your thoughts. Constant self-reflection can lead to an unhealthy obsession with your inner world. Sometimes, it's essential to escape your own mind.

I refer to this as "turning down the volume." It doesn't mean silencing your thoughts or self-talk altogether; instead, it involves purposefully diverting your attention elsewhere. Meditation, especially mindfulness of the breath, offers an effective approach.

Meditation creates a space between awareness and thought, you and your self-talk. This space feels refreshing and expansive, a sense of vastness worth exploring. Practicing in this spaciousness is valuable.

Meditation alters your relationship with your thoughts. It allows you to detach from negative self-talk, observing it without judgment. By accepting negative self-talk as neutral background noise, it loses its power to entangle and pull you down.

Surprisingly, meditation also transforms your relationship with positive self-talk. It becomes a neutral aspect of your thought pattern, not something you overly identify with. This neutrality prevents false positivity, fostering a genuine, natural wellspring of positivity within you. You connect with yourself authentically, free from constructed narratives or concepts.

In conclusion, while how you speak to yourself holds significance, it's equally crucial to embrace moments of silence. Listen to the stillness around you. Feel the caress of the air on your skin, bask in the sun's warmth, observe the play of light and shadow, and immerse yourself in the rich array of colors, shapes, scents, tastes, and sensations.

As you transform negative self-talk into positive self-talk and venture beyond, entering the realm of your awareness free from past or future contemplation—simply being in the present—a new dimension of life will unfold before you.

Wishing you the best on this journey!

21

Addendum: Specific Situations

Mistakes

Remember that earlier quote by Nassim Taleb? "A loser is someone who, after making a mistake, doesn't reflect, doesn't learn from it, feels ashamed and defensive instead of enriched with new knowledge, and tries to justify the mistake rather than moving forward."

This idea isn't new; you've heard it countless times: Learn from your mistakes. Perhaps it's become so familiar that you've grown immune to its importance.

However, the truth remains, and it's worth emphasizing the obvious. If you don't constantly remind yourself of these basic principles, you might forget them, and it turns out, these fundamentals are crucial not to overlook.

This is a natural process, and errors are bound to happen. That's perfectly fine. In fact, it's not just fine; it's incredibly valuable. Don't perceive your mistakes as personal failures. Instead, view them as vital feedback from your surroundings. Every mistake carries information that can help you refine your approach before your next attempt.

So, go ahead, make mistakes, extract insights from them, adjust your methods, try again, make more mistakes, repeat this process until you get it right. And then, continue this cycle to ensure your success isn't a mere coincidence. There's a term for this methodology: it's called science.

Embrace this mindset. Make it your inner dialogue. If something didn't work, ask yourself why. Perhaps it's because you didn't use enough of a particular ingredient. Fine, adjust that and give it another shot. This is the recipe for success.

Health and Fitness

We delved into this topic earlier in the section on motivation. Whether we like it or not, humans are inherently driven by social status. The opinions others have of us can serve as powerful motivation, for better or worse. Of course, the direction of this motivation depends on the environment you choose.

Let's consider fitness as an example. You aspire to eat healthily, exercise regularly, shed some weight, and tone your body. Excellent.

Now, envision two scenarios.

In the first scenario, you purchase exercise equipment and keep it at home. You're motivated enough to use the rowing machine daily. However, since you're alone in your basement, there's no one to witness your exhaustion after just three minutes, your struggle to get off the machine, panting and wheezing, and your subsequent collapse on the couch.

In the second scenario, you obtain a gym membership and start going there several times a week. You encounter the same people repeatedly and begin to form connections with them. You find yourself on the Stairmaster, feeling exhausted and on the verge of quitting. But you're acutely aware of the fit, attractive person of your preferred gender on the Stairmaster beside you. You don't want to appear weak in front of them, so you push yourself harder and overcome your resistance to complete a satisfying workout.

As discussed earlier, you are a complex being. One part of you seeks long-term goals (delayed gratification) and is willing to endure short-term sacrifices, such as dieting, to achieve improved health and appearance.

Then there's another part of you that simply wants to indulge in unhealthy foods without restraint.

Yet another part of you desires to lounge on the sofa and binge-watch episodes on Netflix, even when you've allotted that time for the gym.

But there's also a part of you that craves approval and positive opinions from your peers. If you recognize that this motivates you, you can use it to your advantage.

Self-talk can support your goals, but it becomes much more manageable if you establish the right incentives in your environment.

Nonetheless, the self-talk component is essential. You need an internal dialogue that doesn't say, "This is too heavy; I'll drop it," but instead encourages you with, "You can do this, just one more rep! Alright, now another one!"

Rather than thinking, "I'm so exhausted," it tells you, "This isn't so bad; in fact, it's quite invigorating, and you're really enjoying the rush of dopamine. You can keep going for at least another mile."

Wealth and Professional Life

Navigating the realm of wealth is complex because it's intricately tied to social status, and as creatures inherently driven by status, we care deeply about our position in the social hierarchy. When you lack wealth, you're acutely aware of your low relative status, which often leads to diminished self-esteem. This negative self-talk reinforces your situation, making it difficult to break free. Changing requires confidence and motivation, which are hard to muster when you're trapped in a cycle of self-doubt.

Our perception of status is relative, not absolute. Even a multimillionaire can feel inferior among billionaires but superior among less wealthy individuals. Choosing the right social circle matters here. You don't want to be the unrivaled expert, nor do you want to be at the bottom; both extremes hinder personal growth. Surround yourself with peers of similar abilities and status, allowing for slight variations. Learn from them to enhance your own abilities.

Positive self-talk can aid you. Instead of focusing on what you lack, appreciate what you have. It might not be opulence, but even having a sound mind and good health are assets. Use these qualities to work toward your wealth goals. If seeking a raise, remind yourself of your achievements; approach your boss confidently. If contemplating a business venture, recognize your intelligence and potential; set clear goals and go for it. In career advancement, focus on qualities like intelligence, conscientiousness, and agreeableness. Be assertive without being aggressive.

Relationships

In the dating world, confidence is key. Don't just assess yourself; realize you're also evaluating the other person. Rejection is part of the process, so focus on your positive attributes: your looks, intelligence, sense of humor, and more. You're the buyer, not just the seller; be selective. If someone doesn't appreciate your qualities, move on. In established relationships, recognize your worth. If your partner mistreats you, acknowledge your value and leave; you deserve respect.

In a healthy relationship, appreciate your partner's qualities and be positive. However, the most crucial relationship is with yourself. Treat yourself with the same kindness you expect from others. Positive self-talk not only shapes your outlook but also influences your interactions with the world.

www.ingramcontent.com/pod-product-compliance
Lightning Source LLC
LaVergne TN
LVHW020438080526
838202LV00055B/5247